COURAGEOUS Queens

10 UNTOLD STORIES OF HISTORY'S BOLDEST RULERS

ANGELA BUCKINGHAM

ILLUSTRATIONS BY DÉBORA ISLAS

FOR CHRIS,

FROM ANGELA

FOR LISETA,

FROM DÉBORA

Five Mile,
the publishing division
of Regency Media
www.fivemile.com.au

First published 2021

A catalogue record for this book is available from
the National Library of Australia

Printed in China 5 4 3 2 1

THE Queens

Welcome

This is a book about queens – clever, brave, ferocious and fascinating queens. Powerful queens. These women were more than just the wives of kings. These queens inspired loyalty and fought traitors, won and lost wars, were rulers and tyrants, inventors and innovators.

Despite their impressive lives, most of these women's names are little known. While the pages of history are filled with countless tales of men (from the incompetent to the inspiring), much of these ten courageous women's stories remains too seldom told and too long forgotten.

Why?

Well, that relates to the very idea of women with power.

For centuries, the idea of women with political power was a disruptive idea – an unusual idea, an idea that went against tradition and so, it was a troublesome idea.

It was men who usually held power, and not just at the highest ranks. From royalty right down to the lowliest administrator, most political systems were designed for and run by men.

That made the very notion of a woman having political power challenging – not just to those men in the system, but also for the way history would record these powerful women. For many centuries, history was written mostly by men.

It is then really no surprise that history has typically recorded the ten queens in this book in a way that undercut their achievements, misunderstood their motivations or presented them as a quirk in a long history of male rulers.

The historical norm of men as leaders and leaders as men had real-life consequences – particularly for the queens in this book.

On top of the daily pressures of being the ruler, most of these queens had to fudge, blur and even deny what their people believed it was to be a woman, so they could be, and remain, the supreme leader. How each of these queens handled this challenge was as different as the times and places they lived in.

And that is a standout fact – powerful women arise, often against the odds, across the world and throughout time. "Queen" may be an English word and a European title, but powerful female leaders are a global phenomenon. If we want to understand regal women then we have to look across countries, cultures and traditions. So many amazing stories await us.

These stories are important because they do more than just inform us. They shape our imaginations. This is why it is a problem for me that tales of powerful women are still rare.

When I was growing up, not only were women missing from history, but most myths and fairytales had powerful women only as the evil step-mother, the wicked witch or the vengeful goddess. The stories we tell, be it bedtime stories or grand historical narratives, feed into all of our imaginations – and our imagination influences what we expect of power, of women, and, particularly, of powerful women.

Re-shaping how we imagine leaders is an important part of making men and women equal, and helping us to have leaders of all genders and diverse backgrounds.

This is what inspired me to write this book, to research and look for clues about what these queens were really like. So, for me, this investigation had to be about more than just dates, places, names and facts – more than an encyclopaedia entry of what these women did.

We must also use our imaginations, be inspired by facts but not confined by them. That is how we understand what these moments in time felt like, looked like, smelt like – how these women understood their own worlds, their own actions, their battles, and their own power.

This makes for powerful stories, that might change the way we imagine power …

I hope you enjoy them,

Angela

Queen Map

The stories in this collection took place all over the world. The names of regions, countries and towns often change over time. The place names used in these stories are the names that would have been known to the people at the time of the story.

NORTH AMERICA

SOUTH AMERICA

⑩

1.
Hatshepsut

2.
Wu Zetian

3.
Nzinga

4.
Maria Theresa

5.
Lakshmibai

EUROPE

ASIA

AFRICA

AUSTRALIA

6.
Elizabeth

7.
Hürrem

8.
Kalinyamat

9.
Leizu

10.
Nanny

Hatshepsut

THE GAMBLING QUEEN

In ancient Egypt, 3500 years ago, Pharaoh Hatshepsut sent an expedition into the unknown to find the mysterious land of Punt ...

Hatshepsut looks for clues of betrayal. She tries to read the minds of her officials, the generals and priests who report on the state of her country. They stand to attention in the bright sunlight of her palace courtyard.

She watches every facial expression, every drop of sweat, every twitch and thinks to herself: "Who is loyal to me? Who would betray me? Who would lead a rebellion?"

When the sun goes down, her spies slide out of the shadows and report to her.

"There are rich families plotting against you – they want to pay a smaller tribute ... "

"They hate that you promote people from poor families ... "

"They despise you because you are a woman and you are pharaoh."

Hatshepsut grew up as the daughter of a pharaoh and, later, became the wife of a pharaoh. Hatshepsut knows that every pharaoh must be alert to rebellion.

She summons her treasurer to a private meeting. This talented official is loyal. He is from a poor family, and he relies on her for his new wealth.

"Treasurer Nehesy," the pharaoh murmurs, "I have a plan. You are going to the land of Punt."

"The land of Punt?" splutters Nehesy, disbelievingly. "You mean the land of the gods?"

"Yes," Hatshepsut purrs. "It is written that Punt is a land of immeasurable wealth. You will find this extraordinary place and return to me with boundless treasures."

The treasurer is blunt. "My Pharaoh, we don't know if the land of Punt exists."

"That is what is brilliant about my plan," Hatshepsut continues smoothly. "You will find a rich land, any rich land, and you can call it the land of Punt ... you can trade with the land of the gods."

Nehesy is loyal but honest. He shakes his head. "You can't afford a journey of this scale. The number of boats needed, the sailors, soldiers ... You have a war to the north and a war to the south. You are building temples to the gods. Pharaoh, we are emptying your treasury. It will take all your remaining wealth to fund this expedition."

> *Hatshepsut knows every pharaoh must be alert to rebellion.*

But the pharaoh has thought this through. "How much does it cost to fight a rebellion? This expedition will prevent rebellion."

Nehesy speaks in a low voice. "What if the expedition fails? What if I find nothing?"

"I will give you what is required to find what we need." Hatshepsut rises from her throne. "I can either rule as if I am blessed by the gods, or we can cling to power while others try to pull it from us." She arches her back after a long day sitting at work, and pads out of the throne room.

And so preparations for the journey to the land of Punt begin. Together, the pharaoh and the treasurer plan how many sailors will go on the expedition, the food necessary for the crews and the precious items that will be traded.

The expedition will sail across the sea. But to reach the sea requires crossing the desert. Hatshepsut refuses to be stopped by problems. She orders the boats to be built in pieces, so they can be carried across the hot sands.

When the time comes, it is Hatshepsut herself who leads the expedition across the desert. At the beach, the expedition receives blessings from the god Amen. Then the five boats sail off into the unknown.

Hatshepsut returns to her palace on the River Nile. She watches the Nile rise, overflowing its banks, like it does every year. These waters make her land rich for growing crops. The river rises and falls again, and still the expedition does not return. Again, the river rises ...

Hatshepsut's priests mutter: "If the expedition doesn't come back before the river falls then the gods are angry."

Her advisers grumble: "The treasure taken by the expedition has probably sunk to the bottom of the sea."

Her military leaders moan: "What if monsters guarding the edge of the world have eaten all our sailors?"

"Stop worrying!" snarls the pharaoh. "The gods blessed this expedition."

But, secretly, Hatshepsut fears that there is no rich land of Punt, that she has made a terrible mistake, that she sent her loyal treasurer to his doom. So, each day she prays at the temple, asking the gods to bring her expedition back safely.

One morning, as she returns from the temple, she sees a messenger running up the palace stairs. She bids the boy come to her.

He whispers in her ear. "Your treasurer is sailing up the River Nile. You will be pleased with what the boats are carrying."

Hatshepsut praises the god Amen.

She had always planned the unloading of the boats to be a grand show of triumph. At once, she orders everyone, from the poorest peasants to the richest priests, to come to the docks to watch the return of the expedition. Sitting above them all, Hatshepsut watches from her throne.

When Nehesy disembarks, he bows low before the pharaoh. "My Pharaoh, we sailed far, far away to the land of Punt, where we were welcomed as you said we would be. Then we returned west, across the deserts, until we found the River Nile, which led us back to you."

The treasures are unloaded, one by one: precious gold, ivory, ebony and live animals.

The baboons call angrily to each other and the leopards growl, straining on their leads as they walk down the gangplank. Behind them strut strange birds with crowns of their own and glorious orange markings around their eyes. The crowd *ohhs* and *ahhs* in wonder.

The advisers from the Treasury count and list every creature, every item of treasure as it is carried past. The priests' eyes goggle as basket after basket of incense is unloaded. These rare resins and spices are more valuable than gold because of their importance in religious ceremonies.

But, still, there is greater glory to come.

As if they have moved Earth itself, the soldiers carry thirty trees, their soil and roots wrapped in baskets. The trees are the precious myrrh trees – the very source of the perfume and incense used in the temples! These trees will be planted around the holiest of Egyptian sites.

At the end of the procession, Hatshepsut rises announcing, "All of these earthly treasures are for my heavenly father, the god Amen."

She then takes the finest myrrh and rubs it on her skin, which is gilded with fine gold. Pharoah Hatshepsut shines forth above her people.

After the spectacular show, she takes her treasurer aside, welcomes him home and thanks him.

"The treasure you bought back was more than just a festival to unload the boats," she tells Nehesy. "This treasure will allow me to employ more priests to work at the temples and to ensure each temple will have a chief of the fields, chief of the granary, chief of construction, chief of the workshops and more workers. Each worker shall earn a salary from their Pharaoh Hatshepsut."

Nehesy nods. "And so this is how you prevent rebellion."

"Yes," Hatshepsut smiles. "Exactly."

Hatshepsut ruled for more than twenty years. Across that time Egypt grew richer, the river never flooded, there were no droughts, the priests said the gods were happy, the military was successful in controlling surrounding kingdoms and there were no recorded rebellions against Pharaoh Hatshepsut.

Wu Zetian

THE CLEVER QUEEN

*In China, around 1300 years ago, Empress Wu commanded
the largest empire in the world ...*

Empress Wu scowls at the three generals kneeling before her.
"You want more soldiers?"

The generals nod.

"The horse riders to the north attack, attack, attack! So many of
them! Wild! Different clans!" one general blubbers. "Crossing lands
like the wind! Coming from nowhere!"

The old empress interrupts. "Calm down. They don't come from
nowhere. The northerners are always attacking. They have always
been on horseback. What has changed that you need more soldiers?"

The generals can't answer.

Empress Wu coos. "If I order that you shall have more
soldiers – and take more men from their families – what
will you do with them?"

The oldest general now stands up, proclaiming, "We will send them north to fight the wild ones and win!"

"You said that last year!" the empress roars. "Dolts! Every year, you do the same thing, even when it is not working. You send foot soldiers to fight these tribes of horseback warriors!"

Empress Wu rustles her glorious yellow robes, pointing her bony finger at the trembling generals. "How large is your army now? Hundreds of thousands of soldiers? Men do not grow like rice you know. You cannot cut them down and expect more to spring up after the rain! Get out!"

The terrified military leaders scurry away.

Empress Wu sits brooding on her throne, as her secretaries and assistants run in and out. They carry with them scrolls of accounts, requests and notifications from across the empire.

Finally, Wu snaps with irritation. "Prime Minister! We need to talk." She beckons her prime minister, Shangguan Wan'er.

The empress's favourite adviser rises from her writing of proclamations. The prime minister is Empress Wu's closest counsellor, having raised Wan'er as a child. No-one understands the empress better than her prime minister.

The empress storms out of the red-and-gold throne room. Wan'er follows at a respectful distance. The two women pass through the halls of the enormous palace and out to the balcony.

Wu gazes out across her lands.

"To order men to become soldiers is a terrible thing," she mutters. "Imagine, to order a man from his farm to go and fight far away. To leave his family – maybe never to return."

The prime minister says nothing, but she listens.

Empress Wu fumes. "And then every year those monkey generals come, asking me for more men. What we need is more horses! But we don't have the right land to raise enough horses. We can't train enough horse riders. So we have a never-ending war to the north!"

Prime Minister Wan'er quietly states, "Your generals are imperfect, but you need your generals. They control the army. They are loyal to you."

"No they aren't," snaps the empress. "Don't believe that show they put on. They understand power. They support me because the peasants support me. I make sure there is rice for the peasants during droughts. All that rice grown, shipped up the canals and stored in our granaries, dug deep into the ground; those stores of rice are wells of salvation – thousands and thousands of tonnes of rice. That rice is peace. People with full bellies don't overthrow their emperor. My military knows that. Don't confuse my power for their loyalty."

Loyalty is an issue rarely discussed by Wu and her prime minister, because the empress executed Wan'er's father for disloyalty, for treason. It was then that Wan'er came to the palace as a child slave. But it didn't take long for Empress Wu to notice that Wan'er was extraordinarily intelligent.

Wu values intelligence and bravery. And now Prime Minister Wan'er proves she has both, as she dares to correct the empress.

"My Divine Sovereign," she says with quiet confidence, "the generals do speak the truth when they say we must protect our northern border. Those wild warriors attack our trade routes. Our merchants are killed. Their goods are stolen. Without trade we will not be an empire. An empire takes more than rice alone."

The empress says nothing for the longest time.

Wan'er fears she said too much. She suggests that they return to the court.

"No," answers Wu. "We'll return when we have a solution."

"This is a big problem. It will require a very long walk. Shall we go to the gardens?" suggests Wan'er.

The empress nods.

In the palace gardens, the empress stops to watch the young nobles practising archery. An arrow hits the target.

The empress cheers, crowing loudly.

The successful archer swoons when she realises it is Empress Wu cheering her on.

The empress meanders on, through the trees, across the bridge over the lake and along the creek. Her prime minister follows at a short distance.

The trees part, revealing a wide green lawn. Here, two skilled horse riders practise galloping at full speed on their sturdy horses, while hitting balls on the ground with sticks.

Empress Wu is captivated. "These are the finest horses I have seen in a long time. We need horses like these," the empress muses. "Did we raise them?"

The prime minister shakes her head. "No, these animals were a gift of goodwill sent by a clan of horse people that we negotiated with in the north."

The empress queries, "So some of these wild-horse people will negotiate?"

"Yes. Sometimes," the prime minister responds. "Different clans. Different leaders. All waging war against us at different times."

"Fabulous," grins the empress.

This confuses Wan'er.

"Many clans!" hoots the empress. "That is the answer!"

"To order men to become soldiers is a terrible thing."

She turns sharply, with a swoosh of her long yellow robes. "Back to court!" she orders.

The prime minister runs after the empress, chasing her up the palace steps.

At the top of the grand staircase the empress pauses, letting the prime minister catch her breath.

The empress gloats. "I have a solution! We've sent the wrong army to fight these battles. Instead of sending our farmers to fight in the north – let's pay tribes of wild-horse riders to fight other tribes of wild-horse riders!"

The prime minister races down the gold-gilt halls after the empress and pants, "But we will have to pay a lot to make horse riders fight other horse riders. That will take a lot of treasure."

The empress stops and spins around at the entrance of the throne room. Her eyes are shining with excitement as she looks straight at her most trusted adviser.

"Yes," she says, smiling, "exactly, Prime Minister, a lot of gold! Guaranteed gold and silk and jewels if they defeat the other tribes. Let's negotiate that! We can pay them a fortune, and it will still cost less than this terrible war fought by our peasants."

The prime minister nods slowly. "It is an inspired tactic. Use wild ones to control the wild ones."

"That has a nice sound to it," praises the empress. "Prime Minister, you always have had a fine way with words – ever since you were a child."

Prime Minister Wan'er bows at the compliment.

The empress's plan worked. She paid the tribes further north to fight the tribes along the border of her kingdom. She also ordered the construction of forts along the main trade routes, to make trade safer and easier to defend. These two innovations reduced the number of soldiers needed for her army. Across her reign, Wu dramatically cut the cost of her military, while keeping the peace and uniting her empire.

Nzinga

THE CANNY QUEEN

*In the Kingdom of Ndongo, around 400 years ago,
Queen Nzinga fought a gruelling war against the Portuguese,
who enslaved her people. She also had to ensure the loyalty
of her own followers ...*

Nzinga shines in the darkness. She sits glowing in the golden light of a massive campfire.

Her bodyguards march four noblemen towards the old queen. The guards, battle-hardened women, don't push the men or even touch them, but march so quickly that the four nobles sweat and stumble.

The group stops before Queen Nzinga. All bow.

Nzinga welcomes the noblemen as her guests. "Please sit, eat – let's talk."

"But we are not your guests!" protests one of the noblemen. "We are prisoners. We were arrested, forced to come here!"

Nzinga raises an eyebrow. "Really? My guards haven't touched you. Why would I arrest people and bring them into my secret settlement – the place from which I wage war? You are free to go."

The man peers fearfully into the night.

The queen's settlement is surrounded with hidden trenches, caves and traps to protect her from her enemies. It is here that she keeps her supplies, food stores and weapons, so she can feed her army and continue the long war against the Portuguese invaders.

Another man sobs, "But we don't even know where we are."

Nzinga hushes. "You are with your queen. And your queen has invited you because she heard worrying news ... You are not loyal. You support Ngola Hari, that fool stomping around my lands proclaiming himself king."

The four men sitting at Nzinga's feet glance at each other.

Nzinga understands these quick looks as signs of guilt. She is dealing with traitors, but she knows she can't kill them without upsetting the nobles that support her. She needs her nobles' support as she fights the Portuguese.

Nzinga continues. "Don't look at each other, wondering who betrayed you or spied on you. If you are looking for one source of my information, you are fools. This land is my land. My people love me. The animals listen out for me. The plants report to me. Why, even the wind is my messenger."

At just this moment the breeze picks up, rustling the trees, as if the jungle was speaking to the queen. Nzinga chuckles.

"So let's talk together as we eat together," she tells the noblemen at her feet. "What we will discuss is *why*? Why do you four betray me?"

"We don't!" shout the four terrified men.

Nzinga hisses, "Do not lie to me. I was already queen when you were babies in your mothers' arms."

The noblemen are silent. Platters of food are bought out for them. Nervously, the men pick at the feast.

The queen's eyes narrow. "Do you think I should surrender to the Portuguese?"

"No, no, no," stammer the men.

"Should I stop freeing the slaves that the Portuguese steal?"

"No," the noblemen splutter, as they are handed warm drinks by the court servants.

"You have a problem with the taxes I collect?"

The four men shake their heads in unison.

Exasperated, the queen asks, "Then why is it that you support my enemies?"

One of the noblemen admits, "A king, your Majesty. We need a king."

The nobleman next to him adds, "Your brother was king. Your father was king."

The four men agree. "We want to be led by a king, like our fathers and their fathers."

Nzinga laughs. "Your fathers all served me: their queen. Remember, I have lived a long, long time."

"But it's tradition," one of the men insists. "We are men. We want to be led by a king – like our grandfathers were."

All four men nod earnestly, and another pipes up. "Yes. It is the natural way of things. That is why our law says when nobles betray their king, they must die."

"So you would kill another noble who betrayed his king?" confirms the still-smiling queen.

The noblemen warmly agree with Nzinga. They gorge themselves on the food before them.

Nzinga continues charmingly as she questions her hungry guests, "And so what do you believe makes a good king?"

One nobleman licks his lips. "A king has to come from the royal family! And have the support of the court!"

Another man nods as he finishes his meat, "And be rich! And brave! And a great warrior! Be feared by all!"

The last nobleman chuckles as he reaches for the dried fruit.

"And have wives, lots and lots of wives!"

"Ah," says Nzinga amused, "I have no wives."

The four men laugh and Nzinga laughs too.

After dinner, she bids the men goodnight. "Sleep now, rest well, and we'll discuss this more in the morning."

The sun is already up when the four noblemen stumble out of their beds.

In the middle of the clearing Queen Nzinga stands on a platform. Standing around her are her many husbands. Today, there is no military training, no work is being done. Everyone has come to watch a show.

The noblemen rub the sleep out of their eyes, watching as festive women stream out of the thatched buildings carrying jewellery, feathers, and the robes of the court ladies.

The crowd hushes as the queen stands tall, raising her head.

She addresses her people. "These are the changes in my court: from now on my husbands will live with, dress as and behave according to the rules of my ladies-in-waiting."

One of the sleepy noblemen thinks he is dreaming. "Queen Nzinga, your husbands will dress as women?" he calls.

Nzinga nods.

Another shocked nobleman asks, "Will they dance with the women during ceremonies?"

Nzinga nods again.

The next nobleman asks, "Are they to share quarters with the women of the court?"

Nzinga's face hardens. "Yes, and they will behave according to all the rules and customs of my women. They will be honoured and rewarded, but if they do not behave as women and live with my women as women, I will have them killed."

The queen's final statement echoes through the silent, crowded courtyard.

Then the queen grins. She fixes her gaze on the confused nobleman. "Why do you ask? Are you volunteering? Would you like to get married?"

The crowd roars with laughter. The embarrassed nobleman stares at his feet.

As the laughter subsides, the last of the four noblemen blurts out, "But your husbands ... they were soldiers!"

Nzinga nods. "Yes, and who led them into war?"

The nobleman understands. "You, My Queen."

Nzinga proclaims, "A king, a queen, a soldier, a husband or a wife is a duty – not a man or a woman – but a duty. I expect all of you to do your duty as I do my duty."

The queen's voice rings across the settlement. "I fight at the front. I have been waging war against the Portuguese since my brother was king, and learned how to fight from my father who also fought the Portuguese. I will not stop fighting because it is my duty."

The entire court is silent, awed by their queen.

"Now," she continues, "the Portuguese say that Ndongo needs a king. The Portuguese pay for the usurper Ngola Hari. They say he is king. He is not king. He does no duty. He has not been elected king. He is not the son of a king. Would a king submit to his enemies? No!"

The crowd cheers till the ground rumbles. The noblemen are daunted by the fevered support of Nzinga's court.

Nzinga waves the crowd quiet. "But I respect my nobles. They have fought long against the Portuguese as well. If my nobles want a king then I am King. I rule, I have ruled and I will rule as King."

Again, the crowd gives a mighty roar.

Nzinga beams. "My nobles tell me a king needs wives. How else does a king ensure support of his nobles? My husbands are now my wives as I am now King. We all do our duty."

With great ceremony the men on stage are dressed in the clothing of women of the court.

Nzinga's husbands are turned into wives. Wearing necklaces and bracelets, they bow before Nzinga. She thanks them.

She then points to the four noblemen. Her guards escort them onto the stage.

"You wanted a king. Now you have one ... King Nzinga."

"You wanted a king," Nzinga tells them. "Now you have one. King Nzinga. If you are loyal to your king, you will be protected, your people will be protected and the Portuguese punished if they steal your people. But if you are not loyal to your king, your king will know. Your king will hunt you down and kill you ... as you said a king should."

The four noblemen swear allegiance, bowing low before King Nzinga.

In 1657, the Portuguese, exhausted by their war against Nzinga, gave up their claims to Ndongo. Nzinga then worked to rebuild her kingdom after so many years of war. She died peacefully in her sleep aged 82. Nzinga's long rule established the tradition of queens as supreme leaders in her kingdom. In the 100 years after her death, queens ruled for 80 of those years, without needing to become 'kings'.

Maria Theresa

THE CALCULATING QUEEN

*In Vienna, about 250 years ago, Empress Maria Theresa ruled
a vast empire terrorised by a disease ...*

Empress Maria Theresa is gravely ill. In churches across her empire
people bow their heads, praying for the empress. Many in her family,
including three of her own children, have already died from the
dreaded disease – smallpox.

The empress has burned with terrible fever, red blotches appeared
all over her body turning into pus-filled sores and, now weakened,
she can barely breathe.

At the palace they call for last rites. Her priest comes to prepare her
to face death.

The priest enters her darkened room. The old doctors, one tall and
one short, huddle together, whispering in the shadows.

The empress lies on her bed, soaked in sweat, her grey hair across
the pillow. The priest walks over and touches her forehead.

Her eyes snap open. "I'm not leaving yet."

Startled, her two doctors bustle to her side. The taller doctor whips out his thermometer.

"Take that stupid thing away from me," snarls the empress.

The doctor squeaks nervously, "But, Empress, this is the latest invention, so I can tell how hot you are."

The empress struggles to raise her head, but casts her steely eyes on the skittish man. "I know how hot I am – very hot." She softens. "But not as hot as I was."

The doctors grin at the priest. "The empress is going to live!"

The good news spreads through the royal court, the towns and the countryside. Celebrations continue across the empire for months.

But Maria Theresa does not celebrate. She orders all the mirrors to be taken down so she cannot see her own pock-marked face. She is cranky with all at the royal court. There is no dancing, no music and no singing.

After weeks of gloom, her two doctors make a gentle recommendation.

The tall doctor suggests in a high pitch, "Your Majesty might feel better if you ..." Nervous, he stops.

The short doctor in his deep voice attempts, " If you want to fully recover, you could ..."

Finally they blurt out together, "Be grateful you survived."

"Grateful! Grateful!" she barks. "Smallpox is an army marauding around my lands – killing the young, the old and those in between. When one hundred fall ill – more than thirty die. Those who survive are left maimed. Some hideously scarred. Some blind. Some deaf. This is an enemy I cannot see but who kills my people, my own children. This is an enemy that I have no weapons against."

With that, the empress hitches up her black silk dress and waddles away from the two doctors.

So, the doctors are astonished, when only a few days later, they are summoned to court. They don their powdered wigs and their dress coats and rush back to the palace.

In front of an audience of the nobility, the frowning empress interrogates her two doctors.

"How is it that the English can protect their people from smallpox and we cannot?" she asks. "My cousin," she says, shaking a letter, "has written to me about a treatment that stops people getting the pox."

The crowd gasps.

"Apparently," grumbles the empress, "she heard all about it from Frederick the Second. I prefer to learn about such innovations from my doctors and not from gossip."

The royal court is silent.

"Do I need younger men with younger ideas?" the empress snaps.

All the nobles nod in agreement.

The short, barrel-chested doctor requests permission to speak. "Your Majesty, this English process is a dangerous and unpredictable treatment. They call it inoculation. It involves taking the scab of a smallpox pustule, grounding it into a powder then cutting the patient and putting the smallpox residue into the patient's wound."

"That's disgusting!" Maria Theresa snorts. "Disgusting. And stupid. A sure way to catch the pox."

On cue, the nobles groan, echoing the empress's disgust.

The tall doctor pipes up. "A bit complicated as it seems that the patient, in most cases, does get the pox, but it is a mild case. The patient doesn't get very sick and doesn't die. Once recovered, the patient never gets smallpox ever again."

The empress claps her hands. "Not dying is good. We will try it. We will need lots of people to trial this treatment. We need to understand the numbers of dying versus not dying."

"But, your Majesty, with respect," rumbles the short doctor, "people are terrified of the pox and unlikely to volunteer for such an experiment."

Now all of the nobles shuffle backwards, fearing the empress may pick them for inoculation.

But the empress sees another solution.

"Orphans," she orders. "Lots of them. Test it on one hundred children who have not had smallpox and see if it works." The two doctors frown, muttering to each other.

"And ... what if it doesn't?" says the short doctor.

"The children could die," squeaks the tall doctor. "That is a problem. A big problem. A moral problem."

"Moral problem? The pox is a bigger problem. Our biggest problem! I have sent soldiers into battle to defend our lands. I shall send these children into battle against the pox," states the empress firmly. "And if it works they will live free from the terror and pain of smallpox."

The two doctors wring their hands, shuffle nervously and splutter, but say nothing.

The empress continues, "If it works with these one hundred orphans then I too will be inoculated."

"But you've already had the pox and don't need it!" blurts out her short doctor.

Maria Theresa shoots him a fierce look. "And my children, who have not yet had smallpox will also have this treatment."

The whole court is shocked, silent in surprise.

"We fight this disease together," harrumphs the empress, dismissing the doctors.

They back out of the court, bowing continuously as they go.

The doctors send regular updates to the empress about the new treatment for smallpox and her experiment.

"I shall send these children into battle against the pox."

Her mood improves with every report. As the weeks pass, it becomes clear that the orphans are surviving the treatment and the exposure to smallpox.

True to her word, and before the whole court, Empress Maria Theresa and two of her children are inoculated against smallpox.

The court gives her a standing ovation.

But across her empire, in the months that follow, the pox rages on. The empress seethes at the reports from towns and villages that send her numbers of the dead. She reads of schools, markets and ports closed because of the pox, of villages abandoned and of whole families wiped out.

Again, she summons her doctors, blasting the question: "Why are my people not getting inoculated?"

In a solemn tone the short doctor reports, "We are grieved to tell your Majesty that out of every one hundred people we inoculate, two die."

"Bah!" The empress waves a dismissive hand. "We have towns struck with the pox, with piles of dead! Young, old, rich, poor, fat, thin. Do you understand the scale of death? Can't they count! With inoculation two in one hundred is nothing."

"Not to the families of those who die," peeps her timid tall doctor.

The short doctor shakes his head. "The people are still scared."

"I have done it. My children have done it! What more do people need?" The empress stamps her foot and bellows at the court, "I need strong healthy people. My empire is only

as strong as my subjects. It is time to stop smallpox!"

The doctors whisper. "We know not how to convince people to have their inoculation. We tell people the method. They listen politely and then prefer to leave it to God."

"Method? No-one wants to be part of your method!" shouts the empress. "Inspire them! Charm them! What does everyone want?"

There is silence.

"Cake!" proclaims the empress. "That is what this needs."

The doctors are baffled, "Cake? Empress, this is serious business. We are talking about medicine – not dessert!"

The empress turns away from her doctors, instead gesturing to her secretary. "Royal Announcement – the first sixty-five children inoculated are invited to afternoon tea at the palace. The children will be served by me. That's right, the empress herself will serve the children their treats. If they are inoculated!"

News of the extraordinary tea party spreads across the empire, and reports return that there are long queues of people getting inoculated.

The doctors are invited to the palace tea party, but stick together in a corner of the royal sitting room, avoiding the happy chaos. They are surprised to see that right in the centre of this commotion is the empress herself.
She is smiling and laughing, as she serves cake to delighted children.

"Maybe she is kinder than we thought," squeaks the tall doctor, as he helps himself to a sweet.

A rolling bass laugh reverberates from his short friend. "No. She's not kinder than we thought – just more persuasive."

Empress Maria Theresa ruled for another thirteen years as a forceful leader. She sent her favourite doctor to investigate if vampires really existed in Transylvania and also restructured her army, government and education systems.

Lakshmibai

THE DARING QUEEN

In Jhansi, about 160 years ago, Rani Lakshmibai defied the
British East India Company. The British sort to steal her lands
and disinherit her son after the death of her husband,
the Maharaja ...

Rani Lakshmibai stares down at the raging battle. Across eleven days
and nights of fighting, this night is the worst. It is hot. Fires burn,
lighting the battlefield.

There is no water left in the fort. The British attackers have destroyed
the water tanks. Now there is nothing to drink but fear. No-one can
live without water.

Lakshmibai's commanders come running to her lookout at the top
of the fort yelling. "Lost! All is lost!"

She hears commotion at the gates, the fight to the death.

"I can't surrender! They will kill my son!" she shouts. "Fight on!
Fight on! Blow up the ammunition stores! Fire the cannon! We must
save our boy."

The commanders obey her without question. They know the British are attacking because they deny Lakshmibai's son is her child. The boy was adopted. Now the British take the lands of any ruler, any Maharaja, who dies without a son.

After Lakshmibai's husband died, she called upon the British to recognise her ten-year-old son as the next Maharaja. They refused. They invaded.

She would not surrender then. Her son is her son. She will not surrender now.

Lakshmibai runs into the fort. Her youth and years of military training make her fast. She speeds down the corridors, past the gold-gilt rooms to a bedroom. Here, her combat-trained attendants, all women, guard her sleeping boy. She strokes the child's thick dark hair and gently wakes him.

"It is time to leave," she whispers.

The fort shakes with the explosion of cannon fire.

Lakshmibai holds her son's hand. They dash to the stables. People around them panic.

"Calm," demands Lakshmibai. "Saddle up six horses."

"You'll never get out!" despairs one of the stable workers.

"Fight on! Fight on! ... We must save our boy."

"The gates are blocked by attacking British soldiers."

"We will get out," says Lakshmibai firmly. "We'll jump at the lowest point from the fort walls."

At the lowest point, the walls are still taller than two houses stacked on top of each other.

The stable hands are muttering.

"It is too high," says one.

"No horse can jump that," says another.

"It's impossible," another stable hand sighs.

But Lakshmibai continues preparing her horse. "The horses will jump. We leave now or die."

Five soldiers follow her lead and take their horses. They will guard her whatever comes next.

Lakshmibai mounts her horse. Her son is lifted up behind her. The attendants wrap a long scarf around the boy, binding him to his mother. They ride out, followed by their guards.

The six horses are skittish, with the smells of the burning fort and the noise of the cannon. But the smoke hides Lakshmibai and her escape party from the telescopes of the British.

The first rider to attempt the jump is Lakshmibai. She gallops her horse to the wall. Her son's arms wrap around her waist. He squeezes her in a hug of fear as they clatter, faster and faster to the edge of darkness.

Lakshmibai's horse knows her well. Trusting his rider, he jumps the wall. For a moment this feels like flying. They fall, through the night, the smoke and the clamour of war.

Then the horse's hooves hit the ground, hammering faster and faster as he finds footing on the steep slope of the hill.

Soon, the ground levels out to a flat surface. They are off.

Lakshmibai hears her five loyal guards coming behind her. One guard crashes: a thud, a roll, a cry of pain! She can't stop. With four soldiers she escapes into the night.

The horses pound across the dry land. All the way Lakshmibai's son clings to her, reminding her why they are riding, why they must succeed. The dust rises behind them.

They have far to go. It is more than a day and a night of hard riding to get to the nearest rebel forces where they will be protected. Lakshmibai fears it is beyond the strength of her horse. They don't stop to drink, to rest. They are riding against time.

The sun is above them when Lakshmibai hears British cavalry stampeding towards them.

Her son yells, "They're on us. They're nearly on us!"

Lakshmibai hears gunfire, knowing bullets are flying towards her. She can't dodge or outrun bullets. She fears for her son tied to her back.

The British are gaining on them. She motions to her guard. Suddenly, she turns her horse in a tight arch and hurtles headlong towards her enemy.

In a flash, she takes the reins of her horse between her teeth. Her horse, trained for this, bolts forward, losing no speed. Her guards copy her manoeuvre, turning to take on their pursuers.

Lakshmibai slides out a sword with her right hand and a sword with her left. She wields two long shining, sharp blades.

A British soldier charges towards her. He reaches out as if he will snatch her.

No! Lakshmibai slashes her sword, slides it through the soldier. He tumbles to the ground. His horse bolts, bucking as it escapes the madness.

Lakshmibai glances around at her guards fighting the other British soldiers. She must get her son to safety.

Again, she turns her horse. She charges away. On and on, they ride. Only two of her guards catch up to her.

Night falls. Her boy is faint from thirst and hunger, but they don't stop. They gallop on and on. Her son sleeps. She feels his breathing, his head resting against her back. She is thankful that he is so firmly strapped to her.

Her horse falters. She can feel the sweat on his flanks. His mouth is rimmed with foam.

She whispers to her beloved horse, "Ride on, ride on, ride on", and on they ride.

Finally, she sees the walls of the city of Kelpi ahead of them. The rebels guarding the city welcome her. She is ushered inside the city with her two surviving guards.

Lakshmibai unwinds the scarf around her son. The boy is lifted off her horse. She jumps down and wraps her arms protectively around him.

Rebel commanders run out to greet her, desperate for news from Jhansi.

"First water and food for my son," she orders.

As she puts her son to bed, fed and washed, he looks up at her. "I am sorry, Mother – if I was your son by birth the British would accept your rule and not try to steal our lands."

She hugs him tightly. "You will always be my son. The gods see you as my son. Don't believe the British lie. They make war on that excuse. They take what is not theirs. The only reason for that is greed. Your birth cannot affect the nature of our enemy."

She kisses her boy and pulls up the bed covers over his little shoulders.

When her son sleeps, Lakshmibai returns to the commanders to plan the next stage of the resistance.

Less than two weeks later, Lakshmibai was killed in battle. Her son survived, but he never regained his title as Maharaja. Today Rani Lakshmibai is still revered as an early heroine of Indian independence from the British.

Elizabeth

THE CONFLICTED QUEEN

*In the Kingdom of England, around 400 years ago, Queen
Elizabeth refused to marry and provide an heir to her crown ...*

Elizabeth won't get out of bed. The sun is high in the sky but she
rolls over growling, "My whole court can go rot in my chamber pot."

Her ladies-in-waiting fret.

The bed curtain flicks open revealing Elizabeth's most ancient lady-
in-waiting, the wrinkled and ferocious, Lady Blanche Parry. The old
lady waves a piece of paper.

"What is this?" demands the old woman as she reads from the paper.

*"I love and yet am forced to seem to hate!
I seem stark mute but inwardly do prate.*

*I am and not, I freeze and yet am burned,
Since from myself another self I turned."*

The old lady bellows, "In your papers! Your Majesty! What is this?"

"Lines from a poem," mutters Elizabeth, indicating by her tone that the very question is stupid.

"Of course it is a poem!" squawks Lady Parry.

"I wrote it," snaps Elizabeth, "I'd say it is rather good. You should read out the whole piece."

"It matters not if it is good. What matters is that you mope in bed and write sad poetry like a love-sick girl! You are the Queen of England!"

Elizabeth flops back on her pillows. "I am love sick."

The old woman's voice crackles in fury. "Love sick about that French prince! Love sick about that man you called 'Frog'! Love sick about that man who you paid to leave England! You paid him a fortune to leave!"

"Frog was a funny nickname – a sign of affection." Elizabeth hides her head under her blankets.

But Lady Parry is unstoppable. "Nonsense! We were all relieved when he sailed away! You were relieved! You now lie in bed, preventing the working of your court for a man I know you never loved!"

Elizabeth peeks out sadly from under her covers. "Oh Lady Parry! My emotions joust! It is as if my thoughts wear armour, ride horses and charge at each other. I have two fighting feelings. Yes, I was sick of him. He just wanted money for his army, but now he is gone, and I am miserable."

Lady Parry clicks her tongue in annoyance. But in a gesture of kindness she holds out her hands to the queen. Elizabeth allows her ancient lady-in-waiting to help her to her feet.

"If I chose one English lord as my husband, all the other English lords would revolt in jealousy and greed."

Lady Parry motions to the other ladies-in-waiting. It is time to dress the queen.

The wrinkled old woman says very gently, "A sadness this great is not about this one man."

A waiting woman steps forward with a simple, white dress. Lady Parry helps the queen into the dress.

Elizabeth mumbles, "You are right. My sadness is about love itself. I never had the chance to love, to marry."

Lady Parry guides Elizabeth into her corset. The old woman squints as she threads the laces, and reminds the queen, "You are the queen. If you wanted to marry you could have married."

"I could not and cannot marry!" Elizabeth barks back.

Lady Parry just pulls tight on the corset ribbons, but the queen wants her agreement. "Admit it! For all my power as queen I have no choice. If I chose one English lord as my husband, all the other English lords would revolt in jealousy and greed. My marriage would cause civil war!"

At a side table, a lady-in-waiting cracks two eggs into a bowl, separates out the egg whites and whisks them.

"And if I marry a prince from another kingdom, I will destroy our agreements with all the other kingdoms whose princes I don't marry. Then we will also be at war."

Lady Parry tenderly brushes back the queen's hair into a band and motions to the queen to sit down.

Automatically, the queen raises her face and closes her eyes, but she keeps venting.

"At the same time my whole court – every man out there, bowing and scraping, has begged me to get married! Pleaded for me to produce an heir. They still want a king."

The lady with the bowl of egg whites uses a soft paintbrush to apply the egg to the queen's face.

"I hate this goo," mutters the queen.

"But it keeps you beautiful," soothes Lady Parry. "Keeps your skin smooth."

The egg whites harden, tightening on the queen's face, quietening her and allowing Lady Parry to continue.

"Well, you have outwitted them all and not married anyone. Now your court has only you."

Lady Parry motions for egg white to be washed off with rosewater.

The queen whispers to Lady Parry, "And I have only me – I am alone. I'm getting old."

Another lady-in-waiting steps forward. She applies the queen's make-up, a thick white paste made of vinegar and lead, brushed across her face and neck.

"Ha," mutters Lady Parry. "You only feel old because you look back to your youth. Look forward to where you are going. Then, when you get to my age, you'll look back to now and think 'how young I was'!"

The old woman reassures Elizabeth by showing her a bowl of red pigment. "Behold this madder root, it has been ground down to a lovely red. It will make a gorgeous blush – we will give you beautiful cherry cheeks."

The ladies-in-waiting mix warm beeswax with the red pigment, and add a touch of mercury.

They paint the queen's lips bright red.

Black kohl is applied around the queen's eyes.

Another lady steps forward with a tiny vile of liquid squeezed from the berries of the belladonna plant.

The queen tilts her head all the way back as the woman carefully puts a drop in each of the queen's eyes, causing the black centres of her eyes to get larger and larger like deep black wells.

The queen blinks repeatedly as she speaks, "You may be right, Lady Parry, but it is hard to be a queen. It is harder to be an old queen. If I seem tired or weak they will move against me."

Lady Parry regards her half-dressed queen, with her full make-up, but with her hair tied back, in her shift dress with the corset over the top.

The queen shrugs despondently.

The old lady holds out a skirt constructed of hoops and ribbons. "Then go out before your court! Prove you are not tired! Banish weakness!"

The queen steps into the construction of hoops. Lady Parry ties padding around the queen's waist to support her dress. A long, shimmering, silk skirt is tied over the hoop skirt.

"Now into your bodice, and let's attach your sleeves."

As the ladies-in-waiting attach the sleeves to the bodice locking together the tiny hooks, Lady Parry adds, "This is your armour. You talked of jousting. You joust every day. But you do not carry a shield or wear a metal suit. You wear silk and gems. Your dress shines just as much as armour in the sun."

Two necklaces are carried over and tied around the queen's neck. With that, Lady Parry gestures to the waiting women to bring in the queen's wig. The glorious red headpiece is gently placed and pinned to the queen's hair.

Next in the procession, the women bring the ruffs, one large one to go around the queen's neck and two smaller ones for her wrists.

Lady Parry steps back, proud of her work. "You outshine them all."

The queen, fully adorned, stands before her ladies-in-waiting.

Lady Parry bows to her. "You are our queen. Our Virgin Queen."

All the ladies bow to Elizabeth.

"Add some more pearls to my hair," commands the queen. "The pearl – my symbol that I will never marry a man," smiles Elizabeth, "for I am already married to my country".

As the ladies-in-waiting scatter to retrieve the pearls, Lady Parry whispers, "And I will keep your poem safe. Your secrets of love."

The queen smiles again. "Yes I know you will. Thank-you, Lady Parry."

With the extra pearls laced through her wig, the queen orders: "Now we go to court! To joust!"

Lady Parry steps in place behind the queen and the other ladies-in-waiting line up behind her.

When Queen Elizabeth walks forward, they all follow.

Queen Elizabeth reigned for another twenty years, never married and only named her successor as she lay on her death bed.

Hürrem

THE CONSTRUCTION QUEEN

In the heart of the Ottoman Empire, almost 500 years ago, Hürrem Sultan used her great wealth to build mosques, schools, public kitchens to feed the poor, public baths and fountains. But one project meant more to her than all the others ...

Hürrem Sultan hides herself behind the flowering trees and bushes in a garden at the centre of the harem. This courtyard garden is her favourite place for planning, plotting and telling secrets. It is a rare private corner in this very busy harem, home to the women of Sultan Suleiman the Magnificent, ruler of the Ottoman Empire.

The most powerful woman in the harem, the most powerful woman in the empire is Hürrem. Now her adult daughter, Mihrimah, and her kira sit with her, listening to every word she utters.

But for all Hürrem's wealth and power, she needs her kira. Neither she nor her daughter can leave the harem without the sultan's permission. The doors are guarded by slaves.

The kira is different. She is a businesswoman. She can enter the harem and leave the harem because she is not one of the sultan's women, and she is of a different religion.

Kiras usually trade in jewels, silks and perfumes but this kira is pure practicality. Short and round, she is a ball of efficiency and works on Hürrem's most important projects – construction.

The business of the day is Hürrem's next big building project, a hospital.

"This will be a hospital for women," Hürrem explains in soft honeyed tones. "It will be a safe place for old women, poor women and, of course, sick women."

The other two women nod. The kira takes careful notes.

Hürrem quietly continues. "I'm giving the money and farm land to the hospital so the hospital is self-sufficient, now and in the future. The patients must always be treated for free."

These instructions don't surprise Mihrimah or the kira. Such generosity is a tradition of the sultan's family and their religion.

But Hürrem also instructs her daughter in lessons of how the court operates. "The hospital will be a monument to our family's charity, a symbol of how we rule for our people. We must also make sure members of the most powerful noble families are employed in the administration of the hospital so they make money from our projects."

Her daughter, Mihrimah, immediately understands. "This ties the noble families to you and your work, makes them loyal to you, makes your success their success."

"The hospital will be a monument to our family's charity, a symbol of how we rule for our people."

"Exactly," praises Hürrem, a proud mother.

Hürrem moves on, instructing the kira about what she expects from the architect. She has thought of every detail about the entrance, the fountains, the services to be offered by the hospital. Then she adds, "There must be a separate building within the hospital for infectious diseases. This city suffers the plague too often."

This brings Hürrem to the reason why she wants privacy, why they are planning a hospital in the garden. "I will need you to buy the land for our construction."

The kira doesn't catch the change in Hürrem's tone and just nods, speaking rapidly, "This city, in Constantinople! Well, you've built from Jerusalem to Mecca. This hospital will be a gift for the capital of our glorious empire!"

"Yes – in the heart of the city," Hürrem nods and then continues cautiously. "I am thinking near the slave market, where they sell women, near the slave market for women."

Mihrimah and the kira both sharply inhale.

Mihrimah barely whispers, as if she fears the plants are listening. "Mother, you can't build your hospital there. It will remind everyone that you were once a slave. You may be the most powerful woman in the empire now, but everyone will remember that you were once a slave bought from that very market."

"No-one has forgotten that I was a lowly slave," chuckles Hürrem.

Mihrimah presses on. "But if you build your hospital there, they will know that you are not ashamed that you were a slave."

Hürrem answers calmly with a question. "And why would I be ashamed? I was captured and sold. I did neither the selling nor the buying."

The kira interrupts with practicalities. "Your Supreme Majesty, if you make the hospital free, if you put it next to the slave market, it will be full of slave women."

"Precisely. A safe place for slave women, injured or ill without family or friends to care for them," nods Hürrem.

The kira accepts her orders. "It will be hard to get land right next to the market, in the heart of Constantinople."

Hürrem smiles. "That is what I pay you for. Negotiate hard and don't tell the sellers who you are buying the land for."

The kira has her instructions and a lot to do. On Hürrem's command, she is escorted out of the harem by two guards.

Once the kira has left the courtyard, Mihrimah pleads with her mother. "Mother, this hospital will be a monument to remind people how you went from being a slave to your exulted position – that you did it through bearing children and the sultan marrying you. People whisper that you used magic."

Hürrem shrugs. "My singing was magic enough."

"Have you spoken to my father, the sultan, about this hospital?" persists Mihrimah.

Hürrem pierces her eldest daughter with a sharp look. "Of course. He understands the trap we are in better than anyone else."

Now Mihrimah is annoyed with her mother. "A trap? You are not in a trap. You are the most powerful woman in the empire."

Hürrem takes her daughter's hand. "True. But power is not freedom. Your father and I live in a gilded cage. Your father is sometimes called He Who Survived the Sword."

Mihrimah knows that her mother refers to the tradition that every sultan must kill his brothers when he becomes sultan so there is only one line of power, so there is no-one to fight him for the awesome power of the Ottoman Empire.

She understands that is why the sultans have their sons with slaves.

Slaves have no family and so no power. When the new sultan must kill his brothers, their mothers are powerless to protect them.

Mihrimah is appalled. "This is not the way now. You are no longer a slave! Father married you! He broke tradition to marry you."

"And we have four sons. And tradition is heavy. Power is costly. This is the trap that your father and I live in. We do not know if your brothers can break tradition too."

"But what has this to do with the hospital?" blurts out Mihrimah.

The sadness in Hürrem's voice is deep.

"Living in this cage has made me desperate at times, and I have done hard things. This is my attempt to balance the scale. I will do some good, by giving relief to those who suffer more than I do, for the slaves, for those who live in a tighter trap."

Mihrimah feels her mother's grief, but does not know how to answer.

Hürrem rises and walks away alone, leaving the private garden.

Hürrem built her women's hospital next door to the slave market. She died less than ten years later. When Hürrem died, her daughter Mihrimah continued building mosques, libraries, schools and public kitchens to feed the poor. When her father, the sultan, died, her two surviving brothers fought to become sultan – with one brother killing the other.

Kalinyamat

THE TENACIOUS QUEEN

In the Sultanate of Jepara, nearly 500 years ago,
Ratu Kalinyamat fought to protect her trading routes from
the invading Portuguese ...

Ratu Kalinyamat waits, standing under a silk canopy at the port. She loves the heat, the smell of salty seaweed and the noise of the ships creaking as they rock in the sea.

She is young to be a widow, to rule on her own, but since her husband was killed, this has become her favourite place in her whole kingdom.

Today, she watches the inland traders floating their rafts down from the river. Their rafts are laden with forest treasures. She sees the merchant ships moored at sea. And beyond the ships, she admires the long, white-gold beach stretching away from them, where the fishermen push out their little boats.

Different people, different jobs, different lives, all meet here at her port. But the queen of Jepara is not standing under this canopy to admire her harbour.

She glances across at her old admiral standing beside her.

His weather-beaten face is scarred, like bark from an old tree. He is her most important military adviser. He was loyal to her when her husband was attacked, and he has a lifetime of knowledge about boats, shipping and war.

Kalinyamat confides to the admiral. "Today is the first step to war. War is costly."

"Can you live with our enemy?" questions the admiral in his gravelly voice.

The queen shakes her head. "No. This enemy is a python wrapping itself around my kingdom, crushing us."

"Then you will need to convince the sultans to come to war with you. We can't win this war on our own."

Together, the queen and her admiral wait to welcome five sultans. These sultans all rule rich lands, all trade on the seas and all share one religion.

Before long, the first ship appears on the horizon. From its flag, Kalinyamat recognises this ship belongs to the Sultan of Aceh.

More ships follow. Each ruler disembarks with his envoy, bringing gifts to the queen.

In a grand procession, the queen leads the five visiting sultans up to her palace, the centre of which has a glorious carved roof, held up by huge pillars of painted wood and gilt gold. In this central throne room, there are no walls so the breeze slips through, relieving the heat.

Kalinyamat is clear: "We must push the Portuguese out of Malacca."

There is feasting and music, but these leaders know they are not here to celebrate.

Kalinyamat welcomes her guests from the neighbouring lands. "We are together to discuss our common enemy: the invading Portuguese. We are all trading nations. We all rely on our ships, what we buy and sell. The Portuguese come, not to trade with us, but to control us, to make us their servants."

The sultans all nod, agreeing with Kalinyamat. They all know how the Portuguese patrol the shipping routes, using their military to make all other ships pay a fee for the right to sail.

The Portuguese want to rule the spice trade and control who can buy and sell pepper, cloves and nutmeg.

The queen continues. "They don't honour contracts, they refuse to pay fair prices and they steal what they cannot buy."

All the sultans know this is true.

From behind the guests the admiral adds, "The Portuguese are strong because they control the port of Malacca. From this port, the Portuguese control the Strait of Malacca. This corridor of sea is the safest and fastest route for north-south trade."

Kalinyamat is clear: "We must push the Portuguese out of Malacca."

Two of the sultans shake their heads. "It is impossible! The Portuguese protect Malacca with their massive fortress.

They have huge cannons pointing out to sea and a fleet of ships guarding the strait!"

But the Sultan of Aceh shouts his agreement with Kalinyamat. "For forty years the Portuguese have had the upper hand! Forty years ago, they invaded the port of Malacca. How? Because the sultan was incompetent and cruel! It is our responsibility as sultans to beat the Portuguese!"

Another sultan rebuts him. "Yes, but the Sultan of Johore has tried to win back Malacca four times, and failed four times."

"One sultan alone cannot take back Malacca," Kalinyamat's voice rings out like a bell. "We need to work together."

The Sultan of Aceh brags, "I have a letter here from Sulieman the Magnificent, the ruler of the Ottoman Empire! He too promises explosive powders, soldiers and gunners."

With this spirit of confidence, all the sultans promise ships and sailors and soldiers.

Together, they pledge: "During the next dry season we will attack the Portuguese at Malacca!"

Over the next year, Kalinyamat's port is a shipyard. Every day, she and the admiral oversee construction of huge ship hulls. The busy preparations go on through the wet season, and into the dry season.

Weeks pass. The skies clear.

They have to attack now, before the wet season returns.

Kalinyamat receives the news that the other sultans are launching their ships. She inspects her own armada. Before her are forty massive ships, with two large sails on each ship. She beams with pride at the skill and power of her Sultanate of Jepara.

She thanks the soldiers and sailors who have volunteered: 4000 of her people's strongest, ready to fight and throw out the Portuguese invaders.

She quietly turns to the admiral. "Thank-you, for your knowledge and bravery."

He swells with pride. "All my experience and strength are at your service," he promises. "We will fight hard to bring home glory."

Kalinyamat watches the ships sail out of her harbour. She comforts herself with the knowledge that they will join the ships of the other sultans, a fleet of 200 ships with many thousands of soldiers.

Days pass. Kalinyamat stands at the port. She gazes out to the horizon, willing the return of her ships carrying her soldiers, praying they are victorious.

But the horizon is empty, except for sea birds circling above the water for fish.

Finally, one small ship, a messenger from the battle, sails in with hopeful news.

The armada of the sultans attacked Malacca from the north and have taken control of part of the fort. The battle rages on, with soldiers on land and the ships at sea.

Again, days pass before another messenger comes: the Portuguese are fighting back. They have defeated troops from the other sultanates. Now only Kalinyamat's forces hold out against the Portuguese in Malacca.

Then truly unwanted information comes from the skies: dark, moody clouds rumble in from the north.

Fishermen rush their boats into port. The storm lashes the shore, throwing debris from the sea onto the beach.

Across the queen's beloved port, buildings and storage sheds are smashed till they are no more than sticks. The wet season has come early with a terrible typhoon.

Finally, the storm passes. There is peace on the beach, but Kalinyamat knows this terror came from the north. Her ships are waging war to the north. She fears for her soldiers.

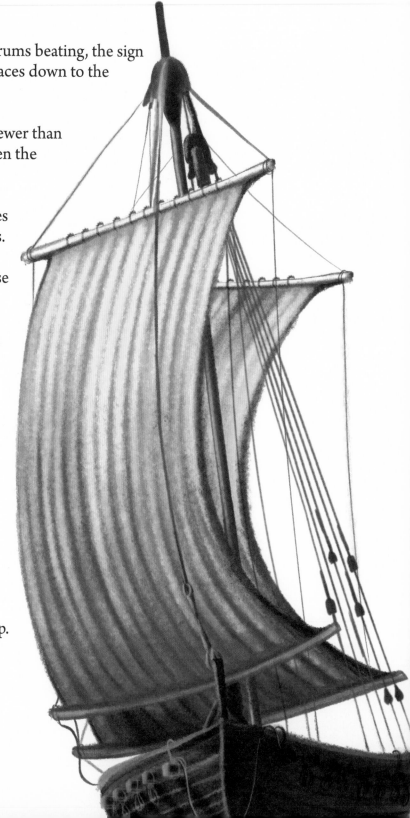

In her palace, Kalinyamat hears drums beating, the sign that her ships are returning. She races down to the harbour.

She counts the returning boats. Fewer than twenty ships cross the line between the blue sky and the dark water.

As the soldiers disembark, she sees suffering written across their faces.

Her chest tightens. The Portuguese have beaten the pride of Jepara.

She scans the lines of soldiers and sailors, realising the old admiral has not returned.

A junior commander steps forward.

"Ratu Kalinyamat, we only retreated once the admiral was killed in battle, after we had lost half our soldiers, after our ships were smashed by the storm."

Kalinyamat grieves the loss of her loyal friend, but she does not weep. She must care for her people.

As the queen bows to her returning soldiers, one soldier apologises.

"My Ratu, my queen. Forgive us for failing you, for failing to defeat the Portuguese."

"None of you have failed," Kalinyamat generously promises him.

"The admiral said the fight would be hard. Other sultans said it was impossible. Against such a foe, resistance, even when it is defeated, is more honourable than surrender. For while we resist, we know who we are."

Kalinyamat continued resisting the Portuguese for her entire reign. She joined with sultans to send a further two armadas to attack Malacca. The alliances of the sultans never beat the Portuguese. Less than twenty years after the death of Kalinyamat rose another great admiral from these sultanates: Keumalahayati, a noble woman from Aceh. She continued the battle against the Portuguese colonialists.

Leizu

THE OBSERVANT QUEEN

In ancient China, nearly five thousand years ago, legend has it that Empress Leizu made an extraordinary discovery ...

Empress Leizu rests under her favourite mulberry tree, looking across her garden, down past the rocky edge of the pond to the lilies hiding a kingdom of frogs. The frogs are quiet now because it is afternoon. They won't call out until this evening.

Behind the pond is the forest, home to a troop of cheeky gibbons. They must be resting, too. None of them venture from the shadows to raid the garden's fruit trees. The empress usually enjoys the antics of these furry little rascals. But now there is only quiet, and today this suits the empress.

She gazes up at the canopy of leaves, seeing jungle green, moss green, grass green, the green of the ground beetle's shell, the green of the praying mantis and the green of snake eyes – all in the green, green, green leaves above her.

Leizu breathes in slowly and out slowly, enjoying the air sliding into her body and leaving again.

She hears her lady-in-waiting set the tea tray down by her side, and pour a cup of tea. Leizu smiles up at her, but doesn't take the tea yet. The tea is too hot.

And so the empress waits, rests. The earth sighs. A slight gust of wind rustles the green leaves above her, shaking free a tiny white cocoon.

The cocoon drops, falling from the branches, down, down, down. It is caught on the breeze and is delivered with a plop into the empress's tea.

As Leizu contemplates her garden, the warm water of the tea gently washes away the glue that holds the cocoon together. When Empress Leizu picks up her cup, she see the threads of the cocoon coming free, unravelling.

Leizu peers into her cup. "What magic is this?" she wonders as the cocoon threads in her tea glisten in the sunlight.

She dips her finger into the cup and swooshes the water around, playing with the shimmering strands, further unravelling in her tiny currents.

Leizu lifts out the thread, pulling it away from the cocoon, unwinding loop over exquisite loop. Out of the warm water, the thread continues to shine, catching and reflecting the sun.

Leizu lifts out the thread, pulling it away from the cocoon, unwinding loop over exquisite loop.

The empress unwinds the thread until nothing is left of the cocoon. At its centre, she finds the creature who spun this thread. Leizu immediately understands where this magic comes from.

Across the garden, her ladies-in-waiting watch on with shocked faces as their young empress stands up, hoicks up her gown, grabs onto two tree branches and lifts herself up into the green canopy.

On dainty feet, her ladies-in-waiting run across to the empress.

At the foot of the tree, they call up to her. "Empress! Empress! What are you doing? Oh please come down. You could hurt yourself!"

"Can't come down, I'm busy!" replies the empress.

High up in the branches, Leizu grins. She has found a fat little caterpillar gobbling the leaves. His stubby green antennae feel his way as he munches through the treetops.

"Hello, my little magician," she whispers to the caterpillar.

The empress then calls down to her ladies at the foot of the tree. She orders them to bring her a basket.

They return speedily with the basket, and Leizu collects dozens of the little white cocoons.

The confused ladies-in-waiting follow the empress back inside. She pledges them all to secrecy, promising that they are about to see magic.

With that, she orders the women to boil a pot of water. As it cools, Leizu drops the basket of cocoons into the pot. The women crowd around as the cocoons reveal their surprise, unspooling their shimmering threads.

The empress fishes out a strand, showing it to her ladies. They all marvel at how the thread glistens. However, the thread breaks and is made of many, many, many fine fibres. Together, the women draw the fibres through a hole in a bamboo tube, turning the threads into one thicker line of string.

It is as if the women are pulling out lines of light.

A little of the remaining glue that the caterpillars used to stick the threads together now binds the fibres into a single thread. The thread is so long, it stretches across the room and out into the garden, on and on and on.

The women stretch out every strand, so they can dry.

One of the younger women asks, "What should we do with this magic string? It is shiny and strong. We could sew with it or embroider or knit."

But the empress has another idea.

She commands
the women to roll the
threads on to a reel, like they
do with wool.

In the following days the empress takes
this magic, shining thread and weaves it
on to her loom.

Click-clack, click-clack.

Leizu creates a fabric that shimmers like a
gemstone, a piece of cloth that holds light.

Only now does the thrilled empress take the fabric to her
husband, the emperor.

He is amazed by the lightweight, shining fabric and
impressed by the strength of the material. He tugs at it
and it does not rip.

The emperor asks his wife, "How did you create this?"

"That is a secret, but I will need a forest of mulberry trees,"
smiles the empress.

And so silk was invented. At first, this precious material was only allowed to be worn by Chinese nobility, but, as years passed, it was worn throughout China. China guarded the secret of silk production for more than one thousand years. The material became more valuable than its weight in gold and gave its name to the trade route – the Silk Road. Silk would dress empresses and queens around the world for many centuries to come.

Nanny

THE RESOLUTE QUEEN

From the hills of Jamaica, more than 250 years ago, Queen Nanny of the Maroons led her people in a long campaign to free slaves exploited by British plantation owners ...

Nanny, Queen of the Maroons, crouches in the jungle, high on the mountain. She is watching the field slaves work in the valley below her.

It saddens her to see the slaves work. Most slaves die here within a few years of arrival. The slave plantation below is a place of cruelty. Nanny notes the whipping post, counts the numbers of overseers and listens to the plantation manager cracking his whip.

Every time that whip crack echoes up the mountain, Queen Nanny feels her anger grow. She sees the redcoats, the British troops sent to guard the plantation.

"Why do they wear bright red coats when they have to fight in the green jungle?" she wonders, counting their guns.

She watches the sun sink between the mountains, the slaves return from the fields, the redcoats drink around their fire, and then all retire to bed.

Now it is deepest night. All is quiet on the plantation below.

Clouds roll in front of the moon, casting the jungle and the fields below into darkness.

Nanny blows her cow horn, her *abeng*. From the horn, a low note swooshes through the night, like a bird hunting.

Below in the valley, on the edge of the plantation, Nanny's people hear her signal, and the jungle begins to move. Out of the mist, the trees and bushes creep forward across the grass, closer and closer to the plantation house.

When they see the long shadow of the nightwatchman, they stop. The jungle is still again.

The nightwatchman walks around the plantation, carrying a flaming torch before him.

Up on the hillside, Nanny sees his flame and thinks him a fool. She knows that a torch doesn't help you see in the dark. Rather, the light blinds you and alerts your enemy to exactly where you are.

When the queen needs to see in the dark she closes her eyes, covers them with her hands and rests a moment. When she opens her eyes, they are used to total darkness and she can see into night, into the shadows.

But this man carries his torch and can only see where the light shines. The nightwatchman's dog, on the lead, is more aware and growls at the surrounding wilderness.

The nightwatchman peers into the night, seeing nothing. He kicks his dog. "Stupid animal!" he grumbles as he turns the corner.

The trees again continue their crawl towards the house.

By the time the nightwatchman has done another walk around the property, the jungle is waiting for him.

As he returns to the corner of the big house, the trees and bushes stand to reveal Nanny's soldiers camouflaged in a uniform of leaves and branches.

One of Nanny's Maroon soldiers steps forward, quietening the dog with a scrap of meat. Then he uses the nightwatchman's own torch to set the house on fire.

Nanny's soldiers run to the small huts across the property to wake the sleeping slaves. Others break into the barns and storerooms to take food and tools.

Nanny watches with pride as her soldiers organise the slaves into small groups and lead them separately to the jungle.

Alarm bells ring across the plantation.

From a cage, a pack of dogs start barking, howling and yelping with excitement.

From the rough barracks closest to the plantation house, Nanny sees the British troops spill out, pulling on their trousers and bright red coats, grabbing their guns.

Men run back and forth. Buildings burn. Nanny watches the chaos.

The slaves clamber up the mountain led by Maroon soldiers. The soldiers bring them to Queen Nanny.

Behind the slaves, she hears the baying dogs. They do not have much time.

The queen considers the faces of men, women and children – their eyes jewels in the night. For them her message is simple.

"You are no longer slaves. You are free. You are free to come with us into the mountains or to return now to the plantation or to strike off on your own into the jungle. This is your moment of choice."

In the darkness one man mutters, "I won't go back – they killed my brother!"

Another voice: "I was burnt by the boiler!"

Another voice: "We are branded like cattle."

No-one chooses to go back down the hill, to return to the horrors of the slave life.

"Okay," Nanny says. "My soldiers, take our new compatriots to our land. Make the river your road, so the dogs can't follow your scent."

The dogs, barking fury, get closer.

A group of twelve soldiers stay with their queen. The other soldiers disappear into the night, some helping the escaping men, women and children, some carrying the captured food and tools.

Nanny orders, "Now let's lead these slave masters and their redcoats on a merry run."

She and her remaining Maroon soldiers set off into the jungle, making sure they are leaving a clear trail. They drop items of clothing and scraps of meat to lay a strong scent for the following dogs.

Barking is never far behind Nanny. This means her plan is working and their pursuers are not on the trail of the escapees.

Up, up, up, higher into the mountains, Queen Nanny leads her soldiers to a ravine, with a narrow path, surrounded by steep rocks on both sides.

"You are no longer slaves. You are free."

On either side of the ravine, her soldiers fade into the jungle. Their camouflage makes them invisible in the dark. They slow their breath, so they are silent and, in the stillness, even the crickets are confident enough to resume their chipping. The night seems at peace.

Hunkered low in the shadows, Nanny peers into the ravine.

The dogs come first, confused, circling around on the narrow path. They leap upwards, unsure how to catch their prey. The plantation overseers with their flaming torches and the redcoats come barrelling up behind the dogs.

There is commotion on the tight path.

Queen Nanny blows her horn. The plantation men look upwards as they are pelted with stones from Nanny's soldiers. The redcoats fire into the darkness, but they can't see their attackers.

Nanny's soldiers draw their weapons and leap down into the ravine. The ambush is short.

The dogs flee into the night. Nanny orders a halt to the fighting when there is one redcoat left alive. She comes down, crouching next to the man. Her voice is low and calm. "You tell your governor what has happened here. One hundred armed men attacked you. Then remind your governor that we are free. We will always be free. We will never accept your slavery. Now go. Run."

Nanny and her twelve soldiers trek back through the jungle and up the river.

As the sun rises, they come to a waterfall where the former slaves and her other soldiers are gathered, waiting.

"We are almost at your new home," announces Queen Nanny.

The escapees are confused. There is nowhere to go.
The jungle around them is dense, and the river itself blocked
by the wall of rock.

Nanny's soldiers grasp the thick vines on either side of the
waterfall and climb up the wet rocks, against the rush of the
water. She and her soldiers help the children, the tired and
the sick.

As they scale the waterfall, they hear music, drumming and
smell the food cooking on big open fires.

The escapees clamber over the edge of the waterfall into
a clearing with many huts, next to the beautiful clear water
of the river. They have arrived at the secret settlement of
Queen Nanny.

They are free.

*Queen Nanny freed over one thousand slaves and
continued her war against the plantation owners and
the British soldiers for almost ten years. Finally, the
British sued for peace. They promised to recognise
the freedom and land of the Maroons.*